LIFE SOLUTIONS

NEVER DENY THE FACT OF LIFE BECAUSE DENYING LIFE MEANS DENYING OUR VERY EXISTENCE UPON THIS PLANET. INSTEAD LIVE LIFE TO THE FULLEST.

JENIL A. GOHEL

This book is dedicated to my parents, for always believing in me, encouraging me to chase my dreams and teaching me to live a meaningful life.

Contents

Acknowledgements

Which things do you need to be thankful to when you have an enormous amount of things that made you do an important thing in life? The most important thing responsible for this book being a reality is "A Mindset" which is actually a sudden idea struck to let people appreciate whatever and however they are and to make their lives the best with the best truthful principles.

Preface

The most important thing that made me write this book is when I saw the people around me that are much more stable be it financially, physically, emotionally, and yet they always remain sad complaining about their miserable life and sorrows. The main intent behind this book is to let people be interested in life again through some simple habits and changes. Then people can see life with more grace, and opportunities and again begin to live it as enthusiastically as our ancestors used to do. The language of the books is not so professoional and people can read it around simply and understand it. The lessons of this book are inspired from others as well as my own personal life.

ONE
WHAT IS LIFE?

Before beginning with the topics and life changes, first of all, let me ask you your point of view on this question - What is Life? Some of you might think that it is the existence of various organisms, some think the way of our existence on earth, etc. which is a universal fact. Discussing only human life because us being the most complex organisms on earth, we function at a whole different level compared to others. We often have heard in our childhood from our elders how they lived their lives. First of all, they didn't have any cellphones, and second of it was that they had love and brotherhood towards each other which today's generation clearly lacks.

So because of a lack of compassion, our personal relations have been damaged as well as we often face more problems. The problems have to be dealt with alone, and sometimes people being so tired and with lack of confidence can't bear a certain problem and sometimes commit suicide or take some other illegal dangerous path. Let us understand this by an example. A student who is working on a science project continuously for 3 months, not attending any functions and maintaining a certain distance with friends and family, fails in that project somehow and gets so upset that he can't even tell his friends or colleagues. In such cases, he often takes some strong steps like suicide. From this example, it can be understood that the student lacked optimism. But one should understand that problems are a part of life and everything be it good or bad, shall pass one day, so there is no point in making sorrow

"If life were predictable it would cease to be life, and be without flavor."
-Eleanor Roosevelt-

The upcoming chapters will clearly show you how can be dealt with various aspects of life.

I have tried to cover up all the aspects of problems faced by we humans in our day-to-day life which are as follows:

- Study and Career prospects
- Love and Relationships
- Mental and Emotional health issues
- Inner peace and happiness.
- Lack of work-life balance

A Positive outlook on the world:

Everyone faces these problems at least once in a lifetime. Be it you, me, or Elon Musk. Jokes apart, everyone has their own sort of problems. No one has walked in anyone else's shoes. The main thing is to deal with these problems with a positive attitude and outlook on the world. How to develop a positive attitude? By releasing all the negative thoughts from the mind by seeing the glass as "half-full" instead of "half-empty". Even if you are not able to get positive-minded by yourself, try listening to some podcasts or motivational speeches. There are an ample number of speeches available on YouTube by JEFF KELLER, Sadhguru, Elon Musk, Jeff Bezos, Bill Clinton, etc. Try reading some motivational books or autobiographies of APJ Abdul Kalam, Swami Vivekanand, Stephen Hawking, and Helen Keller by which you may get to know the point of view of such successful people in their lives. Thus the only way to solve the problems is to have a positive attitude towards the problem believing that "Everything happens for a reason" and also keeping in mind that the sad or happy moment you are going through right now "that too shall pass".

"There is nothing either good or bad, but thinking makes it so." -William Shakespeare

Never think that you alone have the weight of the world on your shoulders. Everyone has to pass through certain difficult stages of their life which are also sometimes unforgettable. So we can understand that people are dealing with a certain set of problems every now and then. The way to tackle it is to behave calmly, positively, and with all the faith in the almighty.

TWO

STUDY AND CAREER PROSPECTS.

The most important thing taught to us either by friends or family to us since childhood is to focus on studies and curricular activities to get our future secured. And in fact, we should get the highest or the best results out of our academics. For that, we have to give 12 years and more than that to it. The thing where the people face the backlog here is that they expect to get the highest results among other classmates. Which in turn creates jealousy and depression. Ever since a child starts learning, he is taught about entering a competition amongst his classmates and friends to always get better grades than others. In this process even if he faces defeat or is less successful than his friends, he gets into self-doubt and ultimately the upcoming results or activities are suffered thereby. The solution to this type of problem is a very simple one. Never get yourself attached in this competition. By this, I don't mean to say that we should stop trying or we shouldn't focus on academics, instead, we should get into a competition with ourselves. We should always try to get better than what we were yesterday. Competing with ourselves ultimately raises our chances of success and we gain more and more confidence in the process.

Let us understand this by an example. A girl named Yamini was studying in her 10th grade. She has always been on top till her 9th grade. From 10th grade, as we all know, things start to get complicated and a bit difficult, which some of us are not able to cope with. The same happened to her and she started feeling in confidence and self-doubt and which resulted in her marks getting deteriorated. She then started to listen to some motivational programs and approach a positive attitude and she stopped comparing herself with others. She started to check how was she getting better day by day. Such habits, ultimately resulted in her marks again being good and she could now look at life with the same enthusiasm as she could look at her former grades. The thing taught by this example is that we should always approach an Optimistic attitude to the world in any form of life because without a positive perception, living life will become difficult, and real life can be lived truly without creating a mess from it.

"Optimism is the faith that leads to achievement; nothing can be done without hope." — Helen Keller

Create your own strategies.

Many people try to copy other people's strategies or the way in which other people survive their life because they don't find the correct ways to do so. Copying others might bring success to you for a short time but it will surely get disappear. By copying, I don't mean to say that copying others is bad. Copying others' good habits is okay but when you start copying their daily routines despite creating your own, now that is not advisable.

It's okay if you cant study 6 hours a day as your friend. It's okay if you are weak at Mathematics, on the other hand, your friend is good at it, and it's completely fine if you understand things quite later than others. But the thing is your should always create your own paths and opportunities. Even if you are able to study only for 2-3 hours, study in such a way that everything enters clearly into your mind. Even if you are weak at Maths, try it until you get good at it and never forget to focus on other subjects to gain marks which you might have ost in maths. If your friend is able to wake up early, don't get tensed thinking that you are not able to do so, if you are comfortable at night, that's completely fine. I am trying to make a point that just focuses on yourself, never think about others' or other people's success, just keep getting better than what you were.

"I'm too busy working on my own grass to see if yours is greener." — Unknown

Now considering the career and job sectors, we will always have someone from our workplace doing better than us. We can't change that but we can change the way we carry ourselves by increasing our rate of work and showing our talent on a larger scale. It is not necessary that you should always be at top of your workplace instead when you are ready to accept the fact that you will work harder than this to achieve a specific target or a specific promotion. Let me tell you, the only thing which is in your control is your deed (KARMA), its fruit is not up to you. So just do your karma without thinking of its result. You will eventually get the fruits according to your hard work and dedication. It is also not certain that we always get the desired result. Sometimes we don't get the results that we have desired in our mind, but possessing a positive attitude can help in such situations.

In order to be financially stable, mere working 9-5 in a job is not going to make a lot of money. But one fact is that at initial levels, a small job has to be done in order to gain experience. Along with a job, always try to look for new business ideas and entrepreneurship. Always look for more opportunities and demands in various fields in the world. When you are done with all the searching and information, make a plan, use your savings in a planned manner, arrange your ideas on paper and projectors, (because people nowadays are interested in watching the ideas on paper instead of just listening to them), show it to the worthy people. Even after making all the above arrangements, if you don't get in touch with more and more people, those ideas are completely worthless. If people don't start the conversation, you yourself step up to people and explain to them your strategies because, at the bottom line, someone has to take the initiative or the conversation will never begin, hindering all your ideas and plans. Entrepreneurship not only requires dedication and talent, but it also requires pure perseverance, hard work, and confidence in oneself. The main thing in it is that at the initial stages you will feel humiliated and people won't appreciate your ideas, but constantly dragging yourself to improve more and more will surely give you your desired outcomes and your business will blossom.

"I'm convinced that about half of what separates successful entrepreneurs from non-successful ones is pure perseverance." -Steve Jobs

Once people study and become financially literate, they still can't become financially independent. We can still face obstacles in the way. The five main reasons why financially literate people may still not become financially independent and develop abundant asset columns to produce large cash flow are mentioned below:

- Arrogance or say "Ego"
- Laziness
- Fear
- Criticism

- Greed (which is both an advantage and a disadvantage) We will discuss the first four factors individually along with greed here, criticism will be discussed in upcoming chapters.

Arrogance: Being arrogant in the case of finances seems to be a dangerous mistake. No person would like to interact or collaborate with someone who is egoistic and seems that they are the only one who knows everything in the world. People like to work with companions who respect other people's opinions and are down to earth. So everyone does come forward to work with the ones who know how to listen to other people's ideas and respect them, instead of judging them.

Laziness: Laziness is the worst loophole on the road to becoming successful. The people who have an ample amount of ideas and ways can still be unsuccessful because of their laziness. Being lazy doesn't allow them to step out of their comfort zone and take some steps to accomplish their goals and ultimately they end up complaining about their conditions and not being able to accomplish their goals. One of the most common examples of being lazy (which will seem controversial to some people), is staying too busy. Too busy to take care of your health, wealth, relationships, and future planning. Therefore never be lazy towards your future and finances or any task which you want to accomplish.

Fear: Fear is the most common problem faced by everyone before beginning a task. Before starting a business, we fear whether it will be liked and supported by everyone or not. If you are a student, there is a fear that whether will be able to secure good marks or not. So there are these types of fears in everyone's mind before beginning any task. But by this, we cant just hinder our practices to it. Despite having fear, we should do our work with full confidence and apply all our resources to it. The result will be either a success or a failure. If it is a success, then congratulations. Even if it is a failure, congratulations again because failure is nothing but a part of the road to success. Failure teaches us how to avoid the mistakes made by us in our past trials when we give it another shot. Failures make us mentally prepared to face such situations without disturbing our mental peace. Whether it is a failure or something bad happened to you, you should be so strong mentally with a positive attitude that your mental peace shouldn't be disturbed. In any kind of situation, good or bad, your mental peace and inner happiness should be it as it. So never allow fear to be a hurdle in your path to success.

Greed: Many times you have heard not to be so greedy because it won't let you succeed. To some extent, it is correct because greed ultimately creates hatred and jealousy towards someone if they get higher results than us. But to a specific extent, it sometimes proves beneficial. There was a student named Mike who just got defeated in a volleyball match. His coaches, friends, and colleagues advised him to quit the sport but he thought that "How can I afford never to play it again?" His mind started running out of solutions, but the hardest part he thought was to fight against the old dogma that tried to instill guilt to suppress such "greed". Without a little greed, the desire to achieve better and higher results cannot be achieved. The world progresses day by day because we humans have a desire in our hearts to proceed towards a better life. New technologies are invented because we desire a better life.

"A little greed can help spur you on, whereas too much greed proves to be harmful." -Rich Dad, Poor Dad (ROBERT KIYOSAKI)

Just remember thata failure quicklygets to our hearts, but success goes to our heads. Our character is revealed at our highs and lows. Be humble at the top. Be faithful in the valleys. We judge ourselves by our ideas. And others by their actions. Be a person who others want to meet and be around. To experience the benefits of something in life, we have to accept the cost. Rewards and risks go hand in hand. Ask yourself "What am I willing to give up to achieve what I want?"

Best destinations can't be reached without going down difficult paths.

The most important thing, in any field, is your hard work. Nothing, I repeat nothing can be achieved without it, even if you are so talented or intelligent. Putting all your efforts in a specific direction with proper guidance can take you to your desired destination. Proper guidance is necessary because we don't know each and everything on this earth. So guidance from experienced people is it our elders, teachers, colleagues, or friends should always be taken before beginning a task so that we can have maximum information about the task. Guidance should be in such a way that it creates a maximum number of new thoughts and ideas in your mind. But in all this mess, never forget to live your life. Yes, you do focus on studies and earning money, but at least give some time to yourself in which you can make yourself better at physical as well as mental levels. Meditate enough, maintain good relations with your neighbors and relatives, give enough time to your family, and exercise regularly, to keep your body and mind clean and healthy. Never get too busy in something because of which your mental peace and inner happiness get affected.

"Success is no accident. It is hard work, perseverance, learning, studying, sacrifice, and most of all, love of what you are doing or learning to do."
-Unknown

The main point in your path to success is your mind, the most powerful tool we have dominion over. Every one of us has the choice of what we put in our brain once we are mature enough. The thing is that instead of saving your money, try to invest it somewhere. Because poor people spend what they earn, middle-class people save what they earn, whereas rich people invest their money. The primary thing is that invest yourself in education first. To be honest, the only real asset you have with you initially is your mind. Each of us has a choice of what we put in our brain once we are mature enough. You can watch TV programs, read golf magazines, and either go to ceramics class or a class teaching financial planning. Most people simply buy investments rather than first investing in learning about investing. Read that twice. Making a plan without any action further upon it, won't yield any results. You have to give your 100% and more than that in any work that you want to do. There is only one life and if we are not able to succeed at that, there is no point in us surviving in this world.

"Some people want it to happen, some wish it would happen, others make it happen. And you should belong to the third category" -Michael Jordan

•

Your words create a huge difference between you being successful or unsuccessful :

Many of you might be thinking that what impact words create on our life or some of you think that words don't matter in us being a success or failure. But trust me it does. Using the same words constantly creates some reactions in your neuro pathways which consequently affects your life in the manner in which you use your words. For example, a girl named Shalini constantly thinks that she isn't good at computers. She thinks that never in her life could she make at computers. So she doesn't even try to give some attention to it, nor does she tries to take a step forward. So, what do you think will happen to her? Because of her continuous negative thinking, her mind and body will function in such a way that even if she tries small programming, she won't be able to do even a simple thing like that. All because her words created an impact on her life. So the words you say to yourself should be chosen wisely to make your life successful. Words shouldn't be used positively only in the case of ourselves, soft words should be used even while talking to someone. Negative words spoken to someone might be very silly and small for us, but to them, those words hurt them by hurt and sometimes they even find themselves mentally broken. Therefore we should think twice before saying anything to anyone keeping in mind what impact will it create on their life.

"The words can make you, break you, they can heal your soul, they can damage you forever. So always try to use the positive words wherever you go"
-Muniba Mazari

Use every opportunity that life provides you to your own benefit:

Life gives us the opportunities to make ourselves better at several phases of our life. But we can only succeed at some. we even fail at some others. The thing that shouldn't be done is not even trying to perform our best at the given opportunity. Trying and failing is nothing to be guilty about, just be grateful and proud of yourself that you at least tried and you can refrain from doing the mistake we did in the past. Therefore give all of your resources to whichever task you want to accomplish.

"If your body does not think life is tough, you are not doing anything worthwhile. It has to be felt that life is tough. When you go to bed, you should not sleep, you must die. Working the very hard, you will always feel that life is tough" -Sadhguru

"You have to take risks. We will only understand the miracle of life fully when we allow the unexpected to happen. " -Paulo Coelho

Choose your friends wisely.

Friends are a huge part of our human life. For the most part of our daily schedule, we are surrounded by friends most of the time. During school times, we tend to form a "group" or "friend circle" which is carried forward till higher classes or more than that. Friends create an important effect on our life - positively or negatively. We learn from our friends be it ethics, life points of view, study areas, or how to carry ourselves forward in life. Our success or failure is greatly determined by what kind of friend circle we have. You should have such friends who enhance you and encourages you to perform better at your workplace or at your studies. Not those who keep you engaged in silly things like smoking, or talking bad about others, which ultimately reduces your level of thought, and you will see life with lower standards and lower opportunities. By that, you won't even try at opportunities and you will keep on engaging in the above-mentioned chores, which will reduce your chance of getting success. Of course, you don't want that. So whenever you try to make a friend, just try to make out how they are, what kind of thoughts they have in their mind, what are their future plans, are they willing to be friends with you to motivate you or criticize and use you? If you get the answers to all those questions positively, congratulations, you've got a friend. If not, sorry but you need to stop all your relations with that person in order that you would not face any problems in the near future.

"Show me your friends and I will tell you who and how you are." -Vladimir Lenin.

You might have often heard that we should make friends with people older than us. I completely agree with it. Let us take, for example, that you make friends with the people of your age. If you are sitting at a specific place, what would be your conversations over there? Let me tell you. You will talk about the latest-released movies, and songs, talk bad about a boy or a girl in your class and send photos, videos, music, etc. to each other. In short, you won't discuss any productive skills or business and finance-related skills. Instead, if you sit with people older than your, they will at least be able to tell you that all those above-mentioned things are useless and of no use for the future. He will also be able to explain how to manage your time more productively, manage your finances, how to make more money, ethics, business ideas, etc. Therefore try to make friends with people who are a bit older than you. They should be good at life experiences, good at finances, older in age, or good at business. Then and then only, they can teach you things more clearly.

"Find a group of people who challenge and inspire you; spend a lot of time with them, and it will change your life." -Amy Poehler

Friends should be such when you face some sort of defeat or loss in your life, they should be the first ones to console and comfort you. Those friends are like a blessing in disguise. A real friend is the one who is able to read all your emotions even when you are willing to hide them from the whole world. A true friend can see behind your mask even when you are fooling everyone else. And it is not at all necessary that you should have many friends, your friend circle should crave quality, not quantity. It doesn't matter that you have too many friends, the thing that matters is those friends bring out the best in you and support you in the worst kind of situation. ***"Making a million friends is not a miracle. The miracle is to make a friend who will stand by you when a million are against you."*** There are also some friends in your contacts who pretend that they are willing to do anything for you even compromising their busy schedules. Those are your good friends, but as I said before, we need a real friend more than good friends. Therefore respect those friends who find time for you in their busy schedules. But love those friends who never see their schedule when you need them.

"Real friends help you find the important things you've lost.... your smile, your hope, and your courage."

THREE

LOVE AND RELATIONSHIPS

Well, to be honest, this is my favorite topic. Every person on this planet comes through this stage in their life, maybe at an early age or the other way. Love is that stage of our life where we explore the side of ours that we ourselves have never seen. Love is nothing but a form of feelings and compassion that we show to others. It can be of any form. You love your parents, siblings, animals, friends, or some other entity. The person who you love should inspire you to follow your passion and support you in every life situation. Only then it can be regarded as a "True Love".

We also have heard from our parents in our teenage years that we should focus on our careers and not get into those relationship and love situations because they will ultimately distract us and take us away from success. Let me tell you they are completely correct. Parents never want us to fail at any stage and whatever advice they give, there is pure love and pure motive behind it. Their advice can sometimes prove to be incorrect but their motive is never to fail or discourage you. So again coming back to the point, they give correct advice but let me ask you a question. Do you ever get distracted by your parents whom you love to the next level? Obviously no. Then if the person who purely loves you without any hidden motive and can extend your limits to the next level, do you think that he/she can distract you from your goals? Instead, they will go for every way by which they can motivate you to go for your passion, even if it means hurting you. Therefore it is not advisable to leave the person who you love for the reason that you want to focus on your goals. If the feelings are real, you will automatically want to grow with the person who you have decided to spend your life with.

But also by seeing the people around us getting hurt because of a relationship, we often have a thought in our mind for once that what if the same happened to us? Every time we fall in love, we get hurt most of the time in our life. There will be only 5 in 100 people that got the love of their life in the first-ever person whom they got into a relationship with and doesn't get hurt. But most of us already have had the experience of getting hurt in a relationship. Sometimes we get hurt so badly that we even lose the hope of loving someone again and we completely forget 'love'. But, everything happens for a reason. The pain and the hurt you are going through at the present moment, are preparing you to be strong for your upcoming life battles. If a person hurts you, you forget the learning of love and won't be able to love someone again. But whenever there is an exit of the person whom you loved with all your emotions, there is always an entry of another person who will teach you the real love which you forgot with time, will show you how to appreciate this amazing life given as a boon by the almighty and will love you the way no other person could ever do. The thing that we should follow is to never lose hope and life's joyfulness. Hope is the only thing by which we can still see life lively and wait for something wonderful and positive to happen.

"Perhaps we are in this world to search for love, find it and lose it, again and again. With each love, we are born anew, and with each love that ends, we collect a new wound. I am covered with proud scars." -Isabel Allende

Every person has some positive and negative points. No person in the world is completely perfect. ***"We all are perfectly imperfect and that's perfectly alright."*** Therefore never try to find a person who is perfect in every sense and is completely similar to you. Everyone has their own way of thinking. own point of view, own ways to live life. So don't expect the other person to live the way you want them to live. Whenever two people get into a relationship, both of them have to change themselves so that the relationship can be managed properly and the feelings do not change. And trust me, a relationship is not based on love only, it requires proper management, trust, dedication, sacrifice, and respect. Sometimes a sacrifice is so big that it even breaks the relationship. So never crave for the person to change. If they are truly willing to be with you, they will automatically find ways to change themselves just to be what you like them to be. And there is a fact that Clap doesn't take place only with one hand. You yourself also need to sacrifice and dedicate yourself to the other person and change yourself so that you can be a better person for him/her. If people have a different point of view from us, we need to start appreciating them. We just can't tell them that their views are incorrect or they should have similar views to us. No, we start to respect their views and agree with them, not because they are completely correct, but because we think that people have their own different kinds of thought processes.

"A great relationship is about two things: First, appreciating the similarities and second, respecting the differences."

It is not advisable to trust anyone in today's world until and unless you know completely about their intentions and behavior. It is not necessary to believe that your friends can never betray you or use you for their own benefits. Therefore to this problem, a solution is that you should appear unknown to them and act like you are completely dumb to their plan. Appear dumb but try to understand their each and every move and act on it when the required right time comes around. Do not think that your enemies always want that something bad should happen to you. You should know how to use your enemies at times by behaving diplomatically with them. The main factor for any person in a relationship is his/her self-respect. If you find that the other person does not respect you and admires you, and criticizes you at several points, then try to make them understand your value 2-3 times. If, even after that, they fail to do so, please end your relationship. I am not telling that you shouldn't compromise because adjustment and compromise are very much needed in any kind of relationship on this earth. But if you find that it's only you who is adjusting every time, then you need to rethink being in that relationship. Such relationships are toxic. Therefore, know your worth and try to let the relationship go. I know that it won't be easy for you to let go of him/her but sometimes prioritizing ourselves above others is not a bad thing, because at last, only you will be the one supporting and standing up for yourself. The world around is so mean.

"When asking for help or maintaining relationships, appeal to people's self-interest, never to their mercy or gratitude." -48 Laws of Power

But again, I will stick to what I previously said. If you can find the right person, you can move mountains. It's just about the real love and support along with the respect and trust they show in you. Never try to find such people. I mean that never try to find such kind of people in your friends or somewhere else. When it's the right time, god will automatically send someone who is completely made for you. If you are currently in a relationship and feel like you are not getting the sum of the parameters of love, trust, respect, support, etc., they may not be your ideal match. Don't try to do everything on your own. Leave some things for destiny and nature. When destiny plays its part, we get the most unexpected result at the most unexpected time. So never lose hope.

"A great relationship doesn't happen because of the love you had in the beginning, but how well you continue building love until the end."

Again, to work out a healthy relationship, the two most important factors, along with love, are trust and mutual understanding. In a survey conducted in the United States, it was observed that the primary reason for divorces was the lack of people spending time with each other and trust issues. Therefore, always be ready to support your partner in any situation. Maybe sometimes, they even fail to tell you what they are going through but you should never fail to make them realize that no matter what, you are always gonna stand by their side in every situation.

Falling in love is a beautiful thing. But the pronblem is you get attached and beomce possessive about everything you love. If you realize with time everything changes, you will appreciate the people in your life and understand when they are not in your life anymore. Detachment makes you free but attachement makes you suffer. The root cause of suffering in this world is attachment.

FOUR

DEALING WITH MENTAL HEALTH.

I have heard many people complaining about being tired the whole day, stressed up, and mentally very weak. I understand. In the present era, people face a lot of difficulties as compared to the past. Though the working hours of the people have decreased from working whole day in the past to just working 9-5 daily at present, it is observed that people are being more anxious now because of the performance pressures, target deadlines, office works, etc. It is obvious that your thinking process decides what will your actions and life be. Our thought processes decide in which direction our life is heading. Therefore to reduce the stress, the idea is very simple and it completely lies up to you. How we perceive a situation and how we react to it is the basis of our stress. If you focus on the negative in any situation, you can expect high-stress levels. However, if you try and see the good in the situation, your stress levels will greatly diminish. You must learn to control your mind, it should not happen that your mind controls you otherwise every situation will go out of your way and you will end up doubting yourself. Major mental health problems are also seen in the youth. Because of the competition going on in the world, sometimes the child has to face defeats and lower results because of which they get into self-doubt and cannot help themselves come out of it. In situations like that, parents need to play a vital role in supporting the child. Children should be told by their parents that though academics are important, it certainly doesn't mean that they will decide the child's future. A child's future is determined by his/her skills and experience in various fields of their interest. The foremost and the main solution to stress-related problems is management. Management of time, resources, skills, tasks to accomplish, etc. to a larger extent proves to reduce the anxiety amongst people. You must be knowing that how important time is for your own life, and obviously, everyone else's. If you search for the materials on time management, you will find an ample amount of books, around 800-1000 on the online purchase sites or in the library.

"No work is stressful, it's your inability to manage your body, mind, and emotions that make you stressful." -Sadhguru

Don't worry. This too shall pass. Every time you are in some sort of problem, you might have thought why me? Why does it happen to me every time? But let me remind you, all people go through that stage in their life when everything goes out of their way. Maybe at the age of 16 or even at the old age of 60s. Just remember that whatever hell you are going through, is going to end one day, and you would be back to normal. Just try your level best to confront and fight against any worst kind of situation. Leave the rest of the things to time. Time heals everything and it will heal you eventually too.

When you feel disappointed, just remember this: Anything you lost, you weren't supposed to have. And anyone that you lost, wasn't supposed to be around. Simple.

Live in the present. We always stress about something that happened in the past, or something that will happen in the future already happened, and is about to happen, respectively. Just forget your past, no matter what you have gone through, but what has happened, has already happened and we can't change the outcome now. But we can change the way we look at it. Instead of seeing it as a tragedy, see it as a way that brought an enormous change in yourself. **A calm and modest life brings more happiness than the pursuit of success combined with constant restlessness.** The future, as it says, has not yet happened. So are you stressing about something which is not in existence at the present moment? Instead, focus on your present time and try to work harder in your current times so that you can secure your future and your future self can thank you. Stress is not what happens to us. It is our response to what happens. And the response is something we can choose. Remember, what happens with you is 10%, how you take it is 90%.

"Pause and remember: Every single event in your life, especially the difficult lessons, has made you smarter, stronger, and wiser than you were yesterday.."

Don't just try to do all things at once because you will end up creating a mess and not fulfilling any single of them. Stress happens when you feel you have to figure out everything all at once. Breathe. Remember you are strong. You will do it. Just live one day at a time. But, getting stress out of your life takes more than prayer alone. You must take action to make changes and stop doing whatever is causing the stress. You can learn to calm down in the way you handle things. Stress management is life management. If you take control of your stress,your life will thank you for it! Sometimes your old life has to fall apart before yor new life can fall together. So dont hesitate to leave the past in the past. Its not your job to fix insecure people. Its your job to fix the part of you that resonated with their insecurities.

FIVE

INNER PEACE AND HAPPINESS

Well, some of you might find this topic a bit fuzzy and also be thinking that why have I kept it as a major thing? But the most important thing which people crave in the present times is inner peace and happiness. Apart and away from the world and its fake people, just being happy and satisfied with oneself and being completely alone from the universe. This is the remedy to cause reduced stress levels too. You don't have to practice any particular thing for it, just need to do a few common chores which will enhance your enthusiasm. How to be happy and at peace with yourself? Meditate for 15-20 minutes per day which will enhance your thinking process and you will have an increased level of thinking with newer ideas and aims. Read 10-15 pages from a book, apart from your academic books, spend enough time with yourself, admire yourself, motivate yourself to do better things day-by-day, and most importantly, detach yourself from the people around you, certainly do spend time with your family as well. Detachment does not mean that you have to renounce all the worldly aspects or it does not even mean that you just be a saint not doing anything. There is a very good line stated in The Bhagavad Geeta that 'Detachment doesn't mean that you don't own anything, rather detachment means NOTHING owns you. Such a beautiful and powerful statement it is. Whenever we see people owning a lot of things, we easily judge them as being entangled in worldly pleasures. But this is not always true. You can live in the world and still be detached. Because you control things. They don't control you. We always had inner peace and pleasure within us. But it is just lost in the shuffle of the worldly aspects, stress, busy and fast life, etc. So you do not need to establish the inner peace rather you just need to find out it within you and by you.

"Have you ever gone looking for something, only to realize you had it with you the whole time. Internal peace and pleasure are just like that".

There is also a difference between the two stated factors. Happiness is determined, to a large extent, by the things going on around us, positive or negative. Whereas inner peace completely depends on us, in any kind of situation. Whether it is a positive or a negative situation, our mental peace, and inner happiness should never be disturbed. Then and then only we can live life to the fullest and understand the true meaning of life. Peace is the result of retraining your mind process life as it is, rather than as you think it should be. Happiness depends on conditions being perceived as positive; inner peace does not. Adopt the principle of **'Simple living and High thinking.'** By simplifying your life you could find that niche of inner peace that everyone longs to have. But it is not always possible for us to be positive and strong all the time. We all go through a hell of a lot of problems in our life. So it's okay to feel sad, demotivated, annoyed, frustrated, scared, and stressed. Having feelings doesn't make you weak, they make you "human".

"Make inner peace your final destination. Make happiness your life's purpose." -Debashish Mitra

You can find peace not by rearranging the circumstances of your life, but by realizing who you are at the deepest and lowest level. And keep this one thing in mind, never let other people or their opinions destroy your peace or affect your decision. They have not walked in your shoes so they will never realize the value of your idea and its deepness and the motive behind it. You will not achieve the results by just meditating or sitting ideally. You will never find peace and happiness until you are ready to commit yourself to something worth dying for.

"If you have inner peace, nobody can force you to be a slave to the outer reality." -Sri Chinmoy

Choose your goals in life hat are important to you. Never choose life goals because you want to impress others. It is not only time and energy that you invest in your goals but it is your life. Even if today were your last day, you wouldn't do anything else. Your life isn't horrible. Just because things aren't going your way, doesn't mean that your life has no meaning. It just means to be patient, to be bold, and to be courageous, because your breakthrough is almost here!

SIX

LACK OF WORK-LIFE BALANCE.

It has also been reported as the major cause along with the others in people's life. People are so busy with their work, jobs, and businesses that they forget to spend some time with their families. And even when they do, they lack in their working sectors. Therefore it is a must to keep a balance of personal and professional life without mixing each other. Therefore the aim is not to prioritize what's on your schedule but to schedule your priorities. Never get too busy earning money in the process that it might cause you to be away and less compassionate towards your family. The thing is that you will never feel satisfied with work until you are satisfied with life. Spend enough time with your family and loved ones, even if it means sacrificing your office hours. Because you never know, when it becomes the 'last time' spent with them. No one on his deathbed ever said 'I wished I had spent more time at the office.' It was quoted by Jane Park 'When I think about work-life balance, I don't imagine it as a perfect day where I got to spend the exact right amount of time having an impact at work and snuggling with my kids at home. I never achieve that. But over the course of a month, or a quarter, or a year, I try to make time for the people and experiences I value'.

"Work is a rubber ball. if you drop it, it will bounce back. The other four balls - family, health, friends, and integrity - are made of glass. If you drop one of these, it will be irrevocably scuffed, nicked, perhaps even shattered." -Gary Keller

Perhaps, if your personal life is not working out properly, how can you expect your professional life to blossom? Personal and professional life are like the two sides of the same coin and that coin is life. You cannot be truly considered successful in your working life if your private life is in shambles. We need to do a better job of putting ourselves and our family at top of our 'to-do' list. Never get so busy making a living that you forget to make life. Money can buy you the most expensive house, it cannot buy you a home. Money can buy you the most expensive clock, it cannot buy you time. With money, you can buy the most comfortable bed, but not sleep. With money, you can purchase food items, but not your appetite. With the money you can buy insurance, but not safety. Thus stop running behind money. I don't mean to say that don't earn money, it is the need of our life, but just don't make your lifestyle which in turn, affects your personal relationships with your friends and family. Focus on improving your familiar relations and your health - the real wealth. Because when health is absent, wisdom cannot reveal itself, art cannot manifest, strength cannot fight, wealth becomes useless, and intelligence cannot be applied. So many people spend their health to earn wealth, and then have to spend their wealth to regain their health.

"Happiness is the new rich. Inner peace is a new success. Health is new wealth. Kindness is the new cool." - -Syed Balkhi

Be Faithful Towards The Almighty.

The one-stop solution and the most pre-eminent solution to any or all kinds of problems is faith. Being faithful towards the almighty at least gives us hope that things will get better and good times will come. Therefore have a habit of remembering god at least once a day, thanking him for all that he has given to you and also blessing you to achieve your desired results. You may also read your holy books such as THe Bhagavad Geeta for Hindus, Bible for Christians, Guru Granth Sahib for Sikhs and Punjabis, etc. You may be going through some sort of problem every now and then. But you must not forget this one thing dear: A day is like a thousand years to the Lord, and a thousand years are like a day. The Almighty isn't really being slow about his promise, as some people think. No, he is being patient with you and your desired outcomes. Also, it is better to doon one's own righteousness, even though imperfectly, than to do another person's righteousness, even tough perfectly. There are three gates leading to the hell of self-destruction - lust, anger, and greed. Therefore one should abandon all three. You have a right to perform your actions but you are not entitled to the fruits of your action. That person, who gives up all material desires and lives free from a sense of greed, proprietorship, and egoism, attains perfect peace. Thus always believe in the power above science which is the almighty. You can do any difficult tasks, and can also improve your inner peace and happiness. Our fates are in the hands of An Almighty God, to whom I can, with my pleasure confide my own; he can save us, or destroy us; his Councils are fixed and cannot be disappointed, and all his designs will be accomplished.

"When the Almighty has predestined you, there is no one in this physical life or in this world, that can block your blessings or success."

9 798887 047829

Printed by Libri Plureos GmbH in Hamburg,
Germany